A Boy's Book of Prayers

by
Mary Hollingsworth

Illustrated by
Lois Rosio Sprague

OLIVER
NELSON

A division of
THOMAS NELSON PUBLISHERS
Nashville

Text copyright © 1992 by Mary Hollingsworth, 3950 Fossil Creek Boulevard, Suite 203, Fort Worth, Texas 76137

Illustrations copyright © 1992 by Lois Rosio Sprague, 217 West Avenue, Wayne, Pennsylvania 19087

Copyright © 1992 by Educational Publishing Concepts, Inc., Wheaton, Illinois

Scripture quotations are from the NEW KING JAMES VERSION of the Bible. Copyright ©1979, 1980, 1982, Thomas Nelson, Inc., Publishers.

Library of Congress Cataloging–in–Publication Data
Hollingsworth, Mary, 1947–
     A boy's book of prayers / by Mary Hollingsworth ; illustrated by
  Lois Rosio Sprague.
          p. cm.
     Summary: A collection of prayers for boys to use in various situations, including prayers for happy or sad times, prayers for school, and prayers for when they are sick.
     ISBN 0-8407-9170-4
     1. Boys—Prayer-books and devotions—English. [1. Prayers.
  2. Prayer books and devotions.] I. Sprague, Lois Rosio, ill.
  II. Title.
  BV4531.2.H557   1992
  242'.82—dc20   92-3095
                                                                      CIP
                                                                      AC

Printed in the United States of America.
1 2 3 4 5 6 7 — 97 96 95 94 93 92

Contents

How You Can Use This Book

Some things are private, right? There are just some things you can't tell anybody else—not even your best friend. But you really need to talk to somebody. So what can you do?

Here's some great news! You can talk to God. He'll listen to everything you need to tell Him. And He won't tell anyone else—ever.

You can tell Him about things that make you happy or sad. You can tell Him about things that make you afraid or worried. You can talk to Him about problems at school, at home, or with your friends. You can laugh when you talk to Him, or you can cry. He won't mind because He understands.

Talking to God is called prayer. And prayer is what this book is all about. We made it small so you can take it with you wherever you go.

You can take it to school and read it during study hall or before a test or an important ball game.You can take it in the car on trips; it will break up the highway boredom. You can take it on fishing trips to read in a quiet place by yourself. You can even take it to bed at night to help you fall asleep.

This book is private. It's yours and nobody else's. You'll find pages to write on toward the back. You'll find famous prayers that men in the Bible prayed in the middle. And you'll find a prayer log where you can keep up with answers to your prayers.

You're going to like this book a lot. It's your own personal book of prayers. So if your name isn't there already, start by putting your name in the front. Then check out the different parts of the book you can use. God's waiting to hear from you.

—Mary Hollingsworth

A Boy's Book
of Prayers

All About Prayer

What Is Prayer?

Pretend that you're in your bedroom all alone. The door is closed so nobody can hear you. You're in your favorite jeans and shirt. And you're lying on your bed munching some chips and sipping a soda. Something exciting has just happened, and you can't wait to tell somebody. So you pick up the phone and call your best buddy.

While you're telling your friend the good news, you laugh and talk. He's excited for you too. You can tell by his laugh and his voice. He's happy because you're happy. When you hang up, you feel great. It's fun to talk to someone you can trust...someone like you...someone who is happy for you.

That's what prayer is like. It's talking to your best friend in the whole universe—God. You can tell Him anything, and He won't laugh at you or make you feel silly. Your feelings are important to God because He loves you. He will be happy when you're happy and sad when you're sad. He will help you to solve problems and to make plans for the future.

Should Boys Pray?

He'll help you at school, at home, and at church.

Yes, God is always there to answer your prayer calls. And His line is never busy! Just say, "Dear God, I need to talk to You," and He'll be listening to every word.

Is it weak to pray? A lot of boys wonder about that. The best way to find out is to look at some of the men in the Bible who prayed. Here are a few to consider:

•Daniel was one of God's prophets. He was the most important person in his whole nation except for the king. He prayed every day. Even when he knew he might be thrown into a pit of lions for praying, he still prayed. And when he was thrown to the lions, God saved him.

Why? Because he prayed! You see, prayer is a smart thing to do.

- Samson was the strongest man who has ever lived. Before he was born, he was dedicated to God. His hair was both the symbol and the source of his strength. In the midst of defeat, Samson prayed to God for strength to destroy his enemies. God answered his prayer. With his bare hands, Samson toppled the pagan temple. Prayer can help make you strong.

- Moses was the leader of the huge nation of Israel. When the Israelites were running from the Egyptians, they got into trouble. The Red Sea was in front of them, and their enemies were behind them. So Moses prayed to God for help. And when Moses lifted his rod, God made a dry path for the Israelites right through the middle of the sea. Prayer can help you overcome your troubles, too.

When Should I Pray?

Do these men sound like weaklings? No! they were the bravest, smartest, strongest, and greatest men who have ever lived. Why? Because they prayed.

The Bible says we should "pray without ceasing." But how could you do that? You'd never get anything else done, would you?

Let's look at it this way. When can you talk to your best friend? Just about anytime, right? You're walking down the street together, and you think of something you want to say.

So you just say it. You're in the school cafeteria and have something to say. You just say it, don't you? Or maybe you think of something to say while you're playing ball. Just yell it out! You don't have to have a special time to talk to your best friend, do you? Since he's always around, you can talk to him anytime.

Well, you don't have to have a special time to talk to God either. Just say what you're thinking anytime. After all, God is always right there beside you. And He's your friend. So you can talk to Him any old time. That's what "pray without ceasing" means: talk to God anytime and all the time.

What Should I Say When I Pray?

One time the guys who were Jesus' friends said to Him, "Lord, teach us to pray." In other words, they were asking, "Jesus, what should we say when we pray?"

So Jesus gave them a sample prayer to help them. He said,

"Our Father in heaven,
Hallowed be Your
   name.
Your kingdom come.
Your will be done
On earth as it is in heaven.

17

Give us this day our
   daily bread.
And forgive us our
   debts,
As we forgive our
   debtors.
And do not lead us into
   temptation,
But deliver us from the
   evil one."

—*Matthew 6:9-13*

Did Jesus mean that His followers had to pray these exact words? No. He was just showing them the kinds of things they might want to pray to God about. You can pray for food. You can pray for Him to help you do right things. But you can also pray for God to forgive you for wrong things you do and to help you forgive other people who do wrong to you (everybody does wrong things once in a while). And you can pray for Him to help you beat the devil.

The truth is, you can say anything you want to God. Of course, you should talk to Him with respect and honor— after all, He is God! And you should always tell Him the truth about things. You might as well; He already knows the truth anyway. You can't fool God, you know.

19

How Do I Know God Hears My Prayers?

Since God doesn't talk aloud to you, how can you know that He hears you when you pray? Here are some ways to know.

It's in His Book. God speaks to you and answers your prayers through the Bible. So, when you pray to God for help, listen to Him talk to you about that problem by reading His Book.

If you pray for Him to give you a new friend, read what the Bible says about friendship (in the story of David and Jonathan in the Old Testament, for example). When you learn to *be* a good friend, you're sure to *find* a new friend. Then you'll know God answered your prayer by helping you find the friend you asked for.

You get what you asked for. The easiest way to tell is getting what you prayed for. Maybe you pray to God to help you get along better with your mom and dad. Pretty soon you find yourself working harder to be helpful and kind to your parents, and things get better. You got what you asked for, and so you know God heard your prayer.

A friend or family member gives you the answer. Sometimes God uses other people to give you the answer to your prayer. You might ask God to help you decide whether to be in the puppet ministry at church. And before long the puppet director asks you to work one of the puppets. Then you know that God has said, "I'd like you to work in the puppet ministry." He gave you the answer through a friend.

22

Things just don't work out. You pray that God will help you get elected class president at school, but one of the other boys in your class wins the election. That doesn't mean that God didn't hear your prayer or care what you want. It means He thinks it's better for you not to be president right now. His answer this time is no. Because He cares about you, God can't always say yes.

God says, "Wait." There are times when you ask for something that God knows (because He's wiser than you) you're not quite ready for yet. So God doesn't say yes, and He doesn't say no. He is just silent. You may think He didn't hear your prayer, but really He's just saying, "Wait a little while."

Then one day, when you don't expect it, you'll get it. That's what happened to Abraham and Sarah in the Bible. They prayed and prayed for a child, but God didn't send them one. Then, when Abraham was one hundred years old, Abraham and Sarah's first child was born. God had been saying, "Wait."

Will God Always Answer My Prayers?

God may say yes or no or wait. But He always hears you, and He always answers—one way or another. What you have to do is learn how to listen to Him. You listen by reading His Book. You listen by hearing Him speak to you through your friends or family. And you listen by watching what happens in your life. If you listen carefully, you'll hear Him answer your prayers one by one.

A good way to keep up with the answers to your prayers is to use the part of this book near the back called My Prayer Log. You can log in what you prayed and how God answered your prayer just as a ship's captain logs in where the ship has been and where it's going.

Where Should I Pray?

You can pray anywhere! That's the best part of all. You don't have to be in a church building to talk to God. That's because He's everywhere. He's in the ballpark, at school, in your home, in the mall, at the movies, at parties, and at youth retreats. Anywhere you go, God is there with you—just like your best friend.

In the Bible there are people who prayed on mountaintops, in gardens, on rooftops, in the temple, in synagogues (church buildings), and in caves and deserts and rivers. Some prayed in kings' palaces and out under trees. They prayed everywhere!

You can pray to God walking down a country road or standing on top of a huge building downtown. You can talk to God in your room at home or standing in line at the amusement park. Don't worry; He'll hear you and answer every time because He loves you so much.

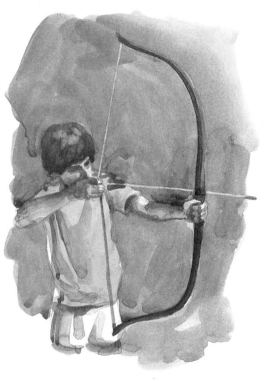

How Should I Pray?

When you read in the Bible about prayer, you find people praying in all kinds of ways. Some people stood up and lifted their faces toward the sky. Some people got down on their knees. Others lay stretched out face down on the ground. Still others lay in their beds.

God doesn't say exactly what position you have to be in to talk to Him. You can pray any way you want.

Think about it. The whole idea is this: You can talk to God anywhere anytime about anything. You can talk to Him everywhere every day. You can talk to Him inside or outside, aloud or silently, standing or sitting or kneeling, laughing or crying, thanking Him or asking Him for things. God's your best friend in the whole world, and He wants to hear everything you have to say.

He loves you and wants to share every part of your life. So why not talk to Him now?

Special Prayers for Special Times

S pecial times in your life require special prayers, don't they? But sometimes it's hard to think of what to say to God at those special times. Here are some prayers to get you started talking to God at those really special times in your life. Once you get started, it will be easy for you to just say what you need to say yourself.

Prayers for Happy Times

Feeling Good

Dear Father, I'm so happy today. The weather's great, school was fun, and I feel good. Thanks for happy days like today, Lord! In Jesus' name. Amen.

Good Grades

Dear Lord, it's a great day! I think I made a good grade on my test at school today, and that makes me happy. Thanks for helping me remember what I had studied. I love You, God. Amen.

Saturday—No School

Dear God, today is Saturday, and I love it. It's fun to have time to do what I want to do. Maybe You and I can just spend some time together today. Thanks for Saturdays, Lord. Amen.

Summertime

Good morning, Lord.
Thanks for summer and
happy times with my
friends and family. It's nice
not having to go to school
every day. I like lying in
the cool grass under a
shade tree and playing ball
and hanging out with my
dad. Help me to remember
to read Your Book often. I
love You, Father. Thanks for
just always being there for
me to talk to. In Your Son's
name I pray. Amen.

Vacation

O Father in heaven, we're leaving on vacation today, and I'm so excited. Thanks for letting us be together and have this chance to enjoy each other. I know we're going to see some wonderful things in Your world. And I guess You can tell that I'm happy today. Please be with us and keep us safe as we travel. And please help me to be patient and kind to the others while we're gone. You're the greatest, Lord! Amen.

Sunshine

Dear God, I'm so glad the sun is shining. It's a beautiful day, and I can't wait to get outside. Your sunshine makes me feel warm inside and outside. It makes the grass look greener and the flowers look brighter and more colorful. Thanks for the sunshine, Lord. You're so kind and good to me every day. I love You for taking such good care of me and my family. And thank You for Your Son. Amen.

Prayers for Sad Times

Friend Is Moving Away

Dear Father, I'm so upset today. My best friend is moving away. I don't know when I'll ever get to see him again. He's such a good friend to me, God. I'll really miss him. Please help me to be brave when he goes. You'll still be there for me, won't You? I'll need You now more than ever. In Jesus' name. Amen.

I'm Moving Away

Dear God, why do we have to move away? I hate to leave all my friends at school and at church. And I'm scared to have to go to a new school and church where we're moving. I don't know whether those new kids will like me. And I don't know whether my new teachers will be nice. Father, help me to know that You'll be there with me no matter where I go. Help me to be brave and even excited about getting to meet new people. I love You, God. In Your Son's name. Amen.

Death of a Pet

O Lord, please help me.
I just found out that my
pet died today, and I'm
really upset. I don't
understand very much
about death. I hope it
didn't hurt when my
friend died. I know
You'll take good care
of this little creature
that You made. I'd really
appreciate Your giving
some special attention to
my little friend. Thanks
for listening, God. Amen.

Parents Divorcing

Dear God in heaven, I really need to talk to You today. My parents are getting a divorce. I guess You already knew that. What will I do now? Our family won't be together anymore. And that makes me so sad. Will You please help me to be strong through this thing? I can't do this alone. Help me to be brave for my parents too. Please help me to understand why this is happening. And help me to know that it's not my fault. Most of all, please just be there when I need to talk to You, okay? Amen.

Death of Mother

Dear Father, help me. I'm so mixed up and sad. I don't understand why my mama had to die. She was so special, and I don't know what I'm going to do without her. Who's going to take care of me? And who's going to teach me things I need to know? Please, Lord, help me to understand why this has happened. Help me to know that You won't leave me too. I need to know that You're there all the time. God, please show me how to help my dad too. We'll need each other more than ever now. Help me, God, and please take care of my mom. I know she's with You now. In Jesus' name. Amen.

Death of Father

O God, why can't I stop crying? My daddy's gone to live with You, and I'm happy for him. But I miss him so much, and it hurts so bad. I can tell that Mom is hurting, too, because she cries a lot. Father, I guess You'll be my only daddy now. I'm sure glad that You're still there for Mom and me.

Please help us to understand why my dad had to die. Show us what you want us to do now. I want to be brave for my mom, but I feel so sad and weak. Please make me strong. Help us to know that everything will be okay as long as we depend on You. I love You, Father. Amen.

Prayers for School

Before a Test

Dear Lord, I have an important test today. I've studied hard, and I've learned as much as I can. Could you please help me to remember what I've studied and learned today as I take this test? With my hard work and Your help, I know I can do just fine. Please be with me today. And thanks. In Jesus' name. Amen.

When I'm Tempted

Father, another kid offered me some drugs at school today. I said no, but it was hard. A lot of the guys really give me a hard time for not trying drugs. And it's not easy to keep saying no, even though that's what I want to do. Please help me to keep saying no, Lord. Make me strong when I face temptation. Help me to remember that Jesus said no when the devil tempted Him. I want to do right, God. Please help me. Amen.

Before a Big Game

Dear Lord, we have a big game today, and You know how important it is to all of us. Please help us to play fairly, Lord, and to be good sports through the whole game. Give us determination and courage. And help us to remember to play the game as Christians should. Please keep us safe from injury as we play, and let the best team win. Thanks for listening, Lord. Amen.

When I Fail

O God, I really messed up this time, and I'm so embarrassed. I didn't do it on purpose, but I feel like such a failure. Please help me to know that everyone messes up once in a while. And help me to do better next time. Father, please let me understand that You love me even when I fail. And I love You too. In Jesus' name. Amen.

When I Win

Dear Lord, I'm so happy! I won today! It feels so good to be a winner once in a while. Please help me to be the right kind of winner. Don't let me tease or make fun of anyone who lost. Remind me that I lose sometimes too. Just please help me to be a humble but happy winner and to enjoy this special blessing from You. Thank You for making me a winner today, Lord. Amen.

When I Compete

Dear God, I want You to be proud of me. We're having a contest at school, and I want to win so much. Several of my friends are entering the contest too. That means that some of us have to lose. Please help me to be fair, Lord, as I compete with the other kids. If I win, help me to be kind about it; and if I lose, help me to be nice about it. Whatever happens, help me to act like Your child. In the name of Christ. Amen.

Teacher Trouble

Dear Father, I got into trouble with my teacher today. I was acting up in class—again. I don't really mean to get into trouble, Lord. I guess I just want somebody to notice me. Please help me to be a better student, Lord. Help me to learn quietly and to be kinder and more helpful to my teacher. Help me to try to be more like Jesus. In His name. Amen.

Talking About Others

O Lord, help me not to talk about other kids in school in a mean way. Teach me not to repeat lies and stories I hear about other students. I don't want to hurt other people, and I know that words can hurt more than anything else. Give me the courage to walk away when my friends start telling stories about other kids. Help me to act as Jesus would act. I pray in His name. Amen.

Prayers for Home

At Mealtime

Dear Father, thank You for the wonderful food that You give us every day. And thanks for my mom and dad who fix it for me. Help me to use the energy this food gives me to do my best for You. And please help me to remember to share my food and blessings with others. In Jesus' name. Amen.

At Bedtime

Good night, Lord. I'm really tired tonight and ready for some rest. Thank You for sleep. Please let the rest I get tonight be enough to see me through the things I need to do for You tomorrow. I pray that You will protect me while I sleep. I love You, Father. Amen.

Trouble with Mom

Dear God, thank You for my mom. She's a really great mom, and I know that she loves me so much. I'm sorry that I sometimes hurt her feelings. We just don't seem to understand each other very well. Please help me to be kinder and more polite to Mom. I really love her, and I want so much for us to get along. I don't want to make her sad. In Jesus' name. Amen.

Trouble with Dad

Dear Lord, why can't I get along better with my dad? He's so important to me, but he doesn't ever seem to have much time for me. I need to be with him more because I love him so much. Sometimes it seems that he treats me like a baby. I know he doesn't mean to; he's just trying to take care of me.

Help him to understand that I'm growing up. And help me to remember that he just doesn't want to see me get hurt. Help me to be kinder to him, and help him to be the kind of father that You are. Amen.

Trouble with Brother/Sister

Dear Father, I'm upset and need to talk to You about it. I'm always getting into arguments with my brother/sister. I don't know why because I really like him/her. We're just different, I guess. We don't like the same things, and we don't do things alike. Please help us to know that it's okay for us to be different and that neither one of us is right or wrong. Help us to learn to look harder for things we can agree on. Please help us not to argue and fight, Lord. In Your Son's name. Amen.

50

Thanks for My Family

Good morning, Lord. I just wanted to say thanks for my family. My mom and dad are really neat people, and I love them a lot. Thanks for letting me be born to such great parents. And thanks for my brother(s)/sister(s), too. We have a lot of fun together most of the time. I really love them, too, even though I don't tell them very often. It's a great family, God! Thanks for giving them all to me. Amen.

51

Prayers for Church

For My Teacher

It's Sunday, Father, and I'm going to Sunday school. Thanks for my teacher at church. He/she really makes our Bible lessons fun and interesting. I know it must take him/her a lot of time to get ready to teach us every week. Please help me to tell him/her thanks. I love You, Lord. In Jesus' name. Amen.

For My Minister

Dear God, thank You for my minister. He's so kind and happy. I really like him a lot. Please bless him and his family, Lord. They work really hard for You, and I know it is not always easy. I'd like to help them somehow if I can. Will You please show me what I can do? Thanks. Amen.

For the Church

Dear Lord, thank You for Your church. There's so much love here, and it feels so good to be with other people who love You. Thanks for giving us the church where we can help each other. I know it really cost You a lot of pain to send Jesus to save us. Thank You for loving us that much. Help me always to live the way You want me to live. And please help me to tell other people about Jesus. In His name. Amen.

Prayers When I'm Afraid

Of the Dark

Dear Father, I'm scared. I sure hope You're there listening to me right now. I don't know why I'm afraid of the dark, but I am. Maybe it's because I can't see what's around me. Please make my heart not feel afraid, Lord. Help me to remember that You're the Lord of the darkness, too, and that You're always with me—night or day. Help me to sleep now knowing You'll take care of me. In Jesus' name. Amen.

Of a Storm

Dear God, I'm afraid of this storm. Please help me not to be so scared. The thunder makes so much noise that I can't sleep very well. And the wind makes scary sounds—it sounds so powerful! Father, help me to remember that You control the wind and the thunder. Make me know that You are the One who tells the storms which way to go. Keep me safe from Your storm, Lord, and help me to be brave. Amen.

Of Being Alone

O Lord, I really hate being alone. I get really scared sometimes when I'm by myself. Please help me to remember that You're always with me, no matter where I am. And help me to know that You're here with me right now; I'm not really alone at all. Keep me safe, Father, and help me not to feel afraid. Stay with me, Lord; I need You. In Jesus' name. Amen.

Of a Stranger

Dear Father, help me. There's a stranger here, and I'm scared. I don't really know what to do. Please help me to remember what I've been taught to do about strangers. Please lead me to safety, Lord. I'm depending on You. In Jesus' name. Amen.

Of Trying New Things

Dear God, please help me to
be brave. I've never done
this before, and I'm afraid I
might fail. I'm afraid my
parents or friends will be
disappointed in me. I really
want to do it and so please
just give me the courage
to do my best. Then,
Lord, would You please
just take my best and
help it along a little bit?
Thanks. With Your help I
know I can do it. I love You.
Amen.

Prayers When I'm Worried

About My Schoolwork

Dear Father in heaven, I'm worried about my schoolwork. I don't seem to be doing very well right now. I'm not sure why. Maybe I haven't really been trying as hard as I can. Please help me not to worry about it so much but to get busy and work a little harder. Then maybe I won't have anything to worry about. In Jesus' name. Amen.

About My Parents

O Lord, I'm so worried about my mom and dad. They don't seem to be getting along very well right now. I hear them arguing and fighting sometimes. I'm afraid they might get a divorce, and I don't want that. Please help them to love each other more, Lord. And help me not to worry so much about them. I know that You can take care of this problem. And...could You please hurry? Thanks. Amen.

About a Friend

Dear God, my friend's in trouble. She's/he's been acting really funny lately. I'm afraid she/he may be taking drugs or doing something harmful. I know it doesn't really help for me to worry, Lord, so could You please show me some way to help my friend? Help me to say something or do something that will help her/him right now. And then help me to believe that You'll take care of the rest. I love You, Lord. In the name of Jesus. Amen.

About a Pet

Dear Father, I'm so worried about my pet. He's/she's so sick right now, and I'm afraid he/she might die. I love him/her so much, God, and I don't want to lose him/her. Will You please take care of my little friend? And please help me not to worry so much but to trust in You instead. In Jesus' name. Amen.

About Someone Who's Sick

My Lord and God, You know that _____ is really sick right now. And I'm so worried. I don't know what to do to help, and I'm afraid of losing her/him. Father, please make her/him well—You're the only One who can do it. And help me to know that You will take care of her/him in the way that's best. I won't worry so much, Lord, knowing that You're on the job. And thanks. Amen.

Prayers of Praise

About God's World

My dear Father and friend, I know You made the whole world and everything that's in it. Your world is so great, God! Thank You for letting me live here and enjoy it. No one else could ever make anything as wonderful as this. I love You and praise Your name with all my heart. In Jesus' name. Amen.

About Jesus

O God of heaven, thank You so much for Jesus. I know that it must have hurt You terribly to let Him die for us. I can't even understand why You would do it for me. I don't deserve it. But I'm so thankful that You loved me enough to allow Jesus to come to earth and save me. You're the greatest, God! And I love You so much. In His name. Amen.

About the Holy Spirit

Dear Lord, I really don't understand very much about Your Holy Spirit, but I want to know Him better. You're so much greater than I am; Your Son is so wonderful; and Your Spirit is so powerful. How can I ever praise You enough for the super things You do for me every day? My heart is so thankful it feels as if it will burst. Praise the name of Jesus. Amen.

About God's Power

Dear Father, I know that You're the most powerful being in the universe. There's no other person or thing that can match Your strength. I bow down before You, Lord, because I respect You so much. And I praise Your powerful and mighty name above anything else in my life. You are the Lord Most Powerful. And I love You. Amen.

Prayers of Thanks

For My Family

Thank You, God, for my family. They're so important to me, and I love them so much. Thank You for my mom and dad, for my grandparents, for my brothers and sisters, and for my aunts and uncles and cousins. Thanks for everyone in my family, Lord. In Jesus' name I pray. Amen.

For Life

Dear Lord, thank You for making me and giving me life. I really love living on Your earth. I love the people I know and the places I go. And I love Your Son Jesus who died in my place on the cross so I can live with You someday in heaven. Thanks for life, Lord. It's great! In Jesus' name. Amen.

For Food, Clothes, and Home

O Father, You've been so good to me. You have given me plenty of good food to eat, nice clothes to wear, and a warm house to live in with my family. Help me to be happy with the wonderful things You've given me. And thank You for taking such good care of me, Lord. I love You so much. Amen.

Prayers When I'm Sick

For Friends

Dear God in heaven, thank You for my friends. They make life so much nicer. We have so much fun laughing and singing and playing together. I know that You especially chose these friends for me to have. And I'm so thankful to You. In the name of Christ I thank You. Amen.

At Home

Dear Lord, I'm not feeling very well today. I have a fever, and my throat's sore. I had to stay home from school. Could You please help me to get well, Lord? I can't do it by myself, but I know that You can do it. Please help me. In Jesus' name. Amen.

In the Hospital

Dear Father, I really hate this hospital. I have to stay in this bed, and there's just not much to do that's fun. Besides, I feel really bad, and my parents are worried about me. Father, could You please help me to get better soon so I can go home? You're the only One who can make me well. And, God, could You please hurry? Thanks. Amen.

Prayers Before I Sleep

After a Good Day

Good night, Father. It's been a good day today. Thanks for happy times at school and at home. I pray that You'll protect me now while I sleep. Help me to rest and be ready for another good day tomorrow. I love You, Lord. And thank You for Jesus. Amen.

After a Hard Day

Dear Lord, I'm really tired tonight. Today was a hard day at school. So please help me to go to sleep right away and to rest really well tonight. Please bless my family as they sleep too. And keep us all safe through the night. In Jesus' name I pray. Amen.

For a Long Time

Dear God, I've been
sick for a long time
now, and You know how
tired I am. My body feels
bad all the time, and I
can't seem to get better.
Could You please make
me well, Father? My
parents and the doctors
don't seem to be able
to do too much. You're
the only One I can turn
to, God, and I know that
You can heal me. I'll be
waiting to hear from You,
Lord. Please make it
soon. In the name of Jesus.
Amen.

For a Busy Tomorrow

Dear Father, tomorrow's going to be a busy day. I'm really excited about it too. I know it's going to be hard for me to sleep tonight, but could You please help me to rest? I'll need to be full of energy tomorrow. So I'd appreciate Your helping me to sleep well and dream happy dreams. Thank You for taking care of me today. In Christ's name. Amen.

For the Whole Family

O Father, please protect me while I sleep. And please bless my mom and dad, my brothers and sisters, and my grandparents. Things have been hard for our family lately, Lord, so would You please help everyone to rest well tonight so that we can get through tomorrow a little better? I love You, Lord. In Jesus' name. Amen.

For Food and Clothes and Shelter

Dear Lord in heaven, You always take such good care of me. You give me food to eat, nice clothes to wear, and a comfortable place to live. Thank You for all these things. And please help me never to forget how much You love me. And, Father, let me be more like Your Son Jesus by sharing my food with others. In His name I pray. Amen.

For All the Wonderful Things

Dear God, thank You for all the wonderful things You do for us every day. Thank You now especially for this food and the energy it gives us. Thank You, too, Lord, for the person who prepared this food for us. In Jesus' name. Amen.

For All the Food We Need

Dear God, You're so good to us all the time, and I love You for that. You've given us all the food we need. But sometimes we take our food for granted and just *expect* You to give it to us. Thank You, Father, for our food and for taking such good care of us. In Jesus' name I pray. Amen.

For Different Kinds of Foods

Dear Father, thank You for all the blessings You give us every day, like the food we have on the table in front of us right now. Help me to learn to eat all different kinds of foods and to enjoy them. And, Lord, thanks for the person who fixed this food for us to eat. I love You, and I love him/her. Amen.

Prayers in the Bible

Talking to God in prayer is nothing new. People have been praying to God ever since He created the world.

The Bible is God's Holy Word. We can learn more about prayer by looking in the Bible. Here are some of the prayers that God put in His Word to help us know how to pray too. You might want to pray a prayer like one of these some time.

A Prayer for Guidance

King David, a man after
God's heart, prayed this
prayer:

Show me Your ways,
    O Lord;
Teach me Your paths.
Lead me in Your truth and
    teach me,
For You are the God of my
    salvation;
On You I wait all the day.

Remember, O Lord, Your
    tender mercies and Your
    lovingkindnesses,
For they are from of old.
Do not remember the sins
    of my youth, nor my
    transgressions;
According to Your mercy
    remember me,
For Your goodness' sake,
    O Lord.

—Psalm 25:4-7

A Prayer for Help

Here's another prayer from King David:

Do not withhold Your tender
    mercies from me,
        O Lord;
Let Your lovingkindness and
    Your truth continually
        preserve me.
For innumerable evils have
    surrounded me;
My iniquities have
    overtaken me, so that I
        am not able to look up;
They are more than the
    hairs of my head;

Therefore my heart fails
    me.

Be pleased, O Lord, to
    deliver me;
O Lord, make haste to
    help me!

—Psalm 40:11-13

A Prayer for Protection

Hear my cry, O God;
Attend to my prayer.
From the end of the
    earth I will cry to You,
When my heart is
    overwhelmed;
Lead me to the rock
    that is higher than I.

For You have been a
    shelter for me,
A strong tower from
    the enemy.

I will abide in Your
   tabernacle forever;
I will trust in the shelter
   of Your wings . . . .

So I will sing praise to
   Your name forever,
That I may daily perform
   my vows.

—*Psalm 61:1-4, 8*

Psalm 23

The Lord is my shepherd;
I shall not want.
He makes me to lie down in green pastures;
He leads me beside the still waters.
He restores my soul;
He leads me in the paths of righteousness
For His name's sake.

Yea, though I walk through the valley of the
    shadow of death,
I will fear no evil;
For You are with me;
Your rod and Your staff, they comfort me.

You prepare a table before me in the presence of
    my enemies;
You anoint my head with oil;
My cup runs over.

Surely goodness and mercy
shall follow me
All the days of my life;
And I will dwell in the house
of the Lord forever.

—*Written by* King David
New King James Version

Prayers to Sing

Do you like to sing? Then these prayers are for you! These are prayers put to music. God loves to hear His children pray and sing. He must especially love to hear them sing a prayer to Him, don't you think? Some of these prayer songs are perfect to share with a friend or your Sunday school class. You can sing them together as you talk to God. You don't have to be a great singer either because God said "make a joyful *shout*" when you sing. He doesn't care whether you have a good voice or not—it's your heart He wants to hear. So tune up and sing a prayer to God.

As Long As I Live

Mary Hollingsworth

Traditional

Dear God up in Hea-ven, I bow down to worship You, to

honor You, my Sav-ior and Lord. I'll praise and I'll

love You as long as I live. Amen. A - men. I'll praise

and I'll love You as long as I live. Amen. A - men.

Father, Keep Me Safe and Happy

Mary Hollingsworth

Traditional

Fa-ther, keep me safe and hap-py through the day and the night.

Fa-ther, help me do the things I know are right _____.

Keep me al - ways in Your sight _____.

Teach Me, Lord

(ROUND)*

Mary Hollingsworth

Traditional

Teach me to be Your ser-vant, Lord; Teach me to share Your Ho-ly Word; Teach me all the Christian joys I've seen and heard.

*HINT: SING THIS ONE AS A ROUND WITH A FRIEND.

Help Me, Father

Mary Hollingsworth

Beethoven

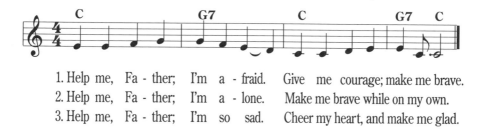

1. Help me, Fa - ther; I'm a - fraid. Give me courage; make me brave.
2. Help me, Fa - ther; I'm a - lone. Make me brave while on my own.
3. Help me, Fa - ther; I'm so sad. Cheer my heart, and make me glad.

Lord, I Love You

Mary Hollingsworth

Traditional

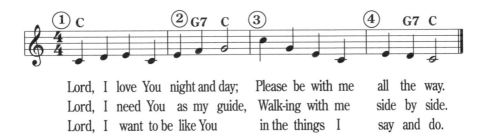

Lord, I love You night and day;   Please be with me   all the way.
Lord, I need You as my guide,   Walk-ing with me   side by side.
Lord, I want to be like You   in the things I   say and do.

Jesus Always Cares

Mary Hollingsworth

Traditional

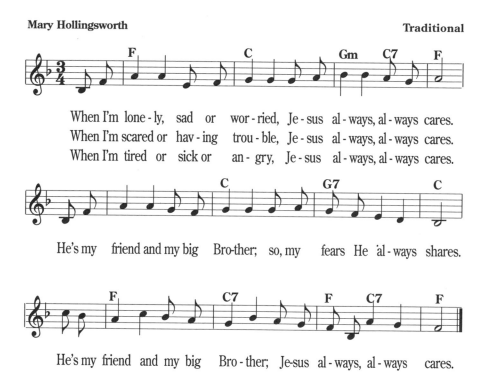

When I'm lone-ly, sad or wor-ried, Je-sus al-ways, al-ways cares.
When I'm scared or hav-ing trou-ble, Je-sus al-ways, al-ways cares.
When I'm tired or sick or an-gry, Je-sus al-ways, al-ways cares.

He's my friend and my big Bro-ther; so, my fears He al-ways shares.

He's my friend and my big Bro-ther; Je-sus al-ways, al-ways cares.

Famous Prayers

People just like you have been talking to God in prayer ever since time began. Some prayers are so wonderful that they have become famous. Here are some of those famous prayers. You might like to pray one of these prayers yourself some time.

Father, We Thank Thee

For flowers that bloom about our feet,
    Father, we thank Thee,
For tender grass so fresh and sweet,
    Father, we thank Thee,
For the song of bird and hum of bee,
For all things fair we hear or see,
Father in heaven, we thank Thee.

For blue of stream and blue of sky,
    Father, we thank Thee,
For pleasant shade of branches high,
    Father, we thank Thee,

For fragrant air and cooling breeze,
For beauty of the blooming trees,
Father in heaven, we thank Thee.

For this new morning with its light,
     Father, we thank Thee,
For rest and shelter of the night,
     Father, we thank Thee,
For health and food, for love and friends,
For everything Thy goodness sends,
Father in heaven, we thank Thee.

—RALPH WALDO EMERSON

Good-Night Prayer

Father, unto Thee I pray,
Thou hast guarded me all day;
Safe I am while in Thy sight,
Safely let me sleep tonight.

Bless my friends, the whole world bless;
Help me to learn helpfulness;
Keep me ever in Thy sight;
So to all I say good night.

—Henry Johnstone

America

Our Fathers' God, to Thee,
Author of liberty,
To Thee we sing.
Long may our land be bright
With freedom's holy light;
Protect us by Thy might,
Great God, our King!

—Samuel Francis Smith

He Prayeth Well,
Who Loveth Well

He prayeth well, who loveth well
Both man and bird and beast.

He prayeth best, who loveth best
All things both great and small;

For the dear God who loveth us,
He made and loveth all.

—Samuel Taylor Coleridge

from *The Rime of the Ancient Mariner*

Jesus,
Tender Shepherd,
Hear Me

Jesus, tender Shepherd, hear me;
    Bless Thy little lamb tonight;
Through the darkness be Thou near me,
    Watch my sleep till morning light.

All this day Thy hand has led me,
    And I thank Thee for Thy care;
Thou has warmed and clothed and fed me;
    Listen to my evening prayer.

—MARY L. DUNCAN

Bedtime Prayer

Now I lay me down to sleep;
I pray Thee, Lord, my soul to keep.
If I should die before I wake,
I pray Thee, Lord, my soul to take.

—Author Unknown

Doxology

Praise God, from whom all blessings flow;
Praise Him, all creatures here below;
Praise Him above, ye heavenly host:
Praise Father, Son, and Holy Ghost. Amen.

—Thomas Ken

The Four Freedoms

God, keep this country free:
    Free from tyrants and their whips
    To stamp out truth and seal the lips;
Free for every race and creed,
    Free from fear,
    Free from need;
God, keep this country free.

—Leah Gale

Jesus, from Thy Throne on High

Jesus, from Thy throne on high,
Far above the bright blue sky,
Look on me with loving eye;
Hear me, Holy Jesus.

Be Thou with me every day,
In my work and in my play,
When I learn and when I pray;
Hear me, Holy Jesus.

—Thomas B. Pollock

Grace

Be present at our table, Lord;
Be here and everywhere adored.
Thy creatures bless, and grant that we
May feast in paradise with Thee.

—JOHN WESLEY

Prayers for Important Days

Special days. Don't you just love them?
Birthdays and Christmas and Easter–they're
the best of all, don't you think? There are
some other special and important days,
too...days like Mother's Day and Father's Day
or Thanksgiving with all the food!

Prayer is a wonderful part of important
days. And the prayers in this section of the
book will help you to talk to God on these
very special days. God never takes a
holiday–He'll always be home when you call
on Him, even on important days.

Christmas

Dear Father, thank You for sending Jesus to the earth to save me. It must have hurt You to let Him leave heaven and come down here. I know that means that You love me a lot. And I love You, too, God, more than anything. Thank You for Jesus. Amen.

Easter

O Lord, it's a great Sunday! It must have been a day just like this when You raised Jesus from the dead. I wish I could have been there to see it. Thank You, God, for bringing Jesus back to life. I know that He lives today and that He is the only One who can save me. Thank You. Amen.

Birthday

Dear God, today is my birthday, and I'm so excited! Thank You, God, for letting me be born. Thank You for making me just as I am. Help me to always live my life just as You want me to. I love You, Father. Amen.

Thanksgiving

Dear Father, this is a special day for us to say thank You for all the beautiful things You do for us. Thank You, God, first of all for Jesus who died to save us from our sins. Thank You for the church where we can meet with other people who believe in You and help each other. Thank You for my family and the love we share.

Father, thank You for my friends and teachers at church and at school. And thank You for our food, clothes, and nice place to live. You're so good to us, God, and we love You very much. Help us to remember to thank You every day. Amen.

First Day of School

Dear God, I'm really nervous today. It's the first day of school, and I'm a little scared. I'm excited to see all my friends again. Will they still like me as much as they did last year? Will I be able to do the schoolwork in this new grade? Will I have a nice teacher? Please help me to be brave, Father. And please make me feel that You're with me today...all day long. I love You, Lord. In Jesus' name. Amen.

Father's Day

Dear Father, I really love my dad. He takes such good care of me and my family. He works hard, but he also has time for us. He teaches me lots of new things, too, Lord, and I like that. Please bless my dad today, Lord. And help me to show him how much I love him. He's a lot like You, I think. Thanks for giving him to me. Please help me to grow up to be a man like him. In Christ's name. Amen.

Mother's Day

Dear Lord, thank You for my mom. She's a great mom, and I love her so much. Help me to show her how much I love her today, God. And please help me to be kind and nice to her every day, not just on Mother's Day. You did a great job when You made my mom, Lord. Thanks! I love You. In the name of Jesus. Amen.

People I Want to Pray For

These next pages are for you to write on. You might like to write down the names of people who need your prayers. That will help you remember to pray for them often.

My Family

Bethie — Sister

Mommy — Mom

Daddy — Dad

Sarah — Sister

My Family

_____

_____

_____

_____

_____

_____

_____

_____

_____

_____

My Friends

Timmy Penwell

Ryan Hughes

Ricky Prater

Jessica Prater

My Friends

My Friends

My Friends

Others

Others

Others

Others

My Prayer Log

This special part of the book is just for you. You can use it just as a sea captain uses his ship's log—to record where you've been and where you're going . . . in your prayers. Each time you pray to God for something special, put down the date and what you prayed for. Then carefully listen and watch for God's answer to your prayer. When you know His answer to your prayer, write in the date and how He answered you. This will help you know that God does answer your prayers.

On This Date	I Prayed For	On This Date	God Answered
	Bethie – lost bike		Bike found
	Daddy - sick or dentist		
	Mommy - when she's sad		
	Sarah - when no one plays with her		

On This Date	I Prayed For	On This Date	God Answered

On This Date	I Prayed For	On This Date	God Answered

On This Date	I Prayed For	On This Date	God Answered

On This Date	I Prayed For	On This Date	God Answered

On This Date	I Prayed For	On This Date	God Answered

On This Date	I Prayed For	On This Date	God Answered

On This Date	I Prayed For	On This Date	God Answered

On This Date	I Prayed For	On This Date	God Answered

On This Date	I Prayed For	On This Date	God Answered

On This Date	I Prayed For	On This Date	God Answered

On This Date	I Prayed For	On This Date	God Answered

My Personal Prayers

These next few pages are where you can write your own special prayers. If you need more room, you might like to get a blank notebook to use. Keep on praying!